Sweetness of the Heart, Mind, and Soul

PETE FRIERSON

Order this book online at www.trafford.com
or email orders@trafford.com

Most Trafford titles are also available at major online book retailers.

Printed in the United States of America.

ISBN: 978-1-4907-3761-4 (sc)
978-1-4907-3762-1 (e)

Library of Congress Control Number: 2014909546

Our mission is to efficiently provide the world's finest, most comprehensive book publishing service, enabling every author to experience
success. To find out how to publish your book, your way, and have it available worldwide, visit us online at www.trafford.com

Trafford rev. 6/13/2014

Trafford
PUBLISHING®   www.trafford.com
North America & international
toll-free: 1 888 232 4444 (USA & Canada)
phone: 250 383 6864 ♦ fax: 812 355 4082

CONTENTS

LIFE

LOVE

FAMILY AND FRIENDS

INSPIRATIONAL

Acknowledgments

This book, ***Sweetness of the Heart, Mind, and Soul,*** is a tribute to my late parents, Clarence and Alma Frierson; my brother, Clarence Frierson Jr.; my nephews Rodney Frierson and Geron Jones; my father- and mother-in-law, J. B. and Hattie Johnson; my brother-in-law, Hosea Butler Jr.; and my friends Harold Leroy Williams, Louise Tidwell, and Dewey and Betty Turner.

Sweetness is also the reflection of God's wisdom passed on to me through the vessel of his knowledge.

The poem "*Why I Write*" shares the insight into why words come to me and I write, not withholding the thought that my writings are meant to be a reflection not of me but of my thoughts.

Special thanks to my dear friend Diane M. McFall for making this book possible. Her efforts have allowed my mind and heart to share *Sweetness of the Heart, Mind, and Soul* with the world.

SWEETNESS

Your appeal is of such sweetness,
it melts the heart,
causes blood to flow from the head to the toe.

Sweetness, something most people aspire for,
yet God gave you a gift and with each
day of your life, I can hear it in your voice,
see it in your eyes and most of all,
that lovely smile that shines no
matter what the time or place.

Sweetness, something that cannot be
purchased from a store,
only from a warm and loving heart.
Your appeal causes one to be thankful
for every moment that we are given
never forgetting to return that sweetness
back to where it all began
and that is with you.

So no matter where you go or who
you are with
never let the sweetness become dull
or bitter because you have so much to give.
For you, dear,
kindness and sweetness
is a virtue of yourself . . .

WHY I WRITE

I write because it gives others the sense of reflection; it gives others a new thought process, a new way of looking at life, a new way of looking at their situation, a new way of doing things. I write because it is an expression of myself, a gift from God, a way to express words like never expressed before. I write because it is an outlet, an outlet to the heart, to the mind, to the soul, to the core of expressing what others cannot express. I write because I enjoy allowing my mind to think and feel how others would feel, and it gives me that chance to express it so others can read it and say, "That sounds like my situation." I write because it can uplift those who are down, it can bring a smile to those who are sad, it can make the heart feel better, and the soul comes alive. I write because it gives me something to do; to see just how far my God will allow me to expand, with all the talents that he gave me. I write to make Him proud. I write to make you proud. I write to make me proud to know that I am making a difference in the world and to your life. I write, I write, and I write.

FANTASY

We all fantasize in this world about this or that.
We may fantasize about a nice house,
nice car, nice furniture, or a nice vacation,
but we fantasize and that's life.

We fantasize about winning the lottery,
going to Las Vegas or Atlantic City,
winning big money.
We fantasize about winning
Publisher's Clearing House Sweepstakes
or winning a big prize,
but we fantasize and that's life.

We fantasize too about love and happiness.
Something that all human beings want,
desire, and have a strong need for.
We fantasize sometimes when we're watching
One Life to Live, All My Children,
As the World Turns,
and *What Hasn't Happened Yet.*
But we fantasize and that's life.

We fantasize about having a big job,
making a nice salary, owning our own
company, spreading our wings,
and living sometimes in a foreign country.
We fantasize and that's life.

Is it okay to fantasize? Yes, it is.
It opens our minds and it keeps us alert
and sharp about the ability to fantasize and dream.
Fantasy sometimes is not more than an illusion
or a sense of day dreaming,
but it's okay to fantasize because it's life.

There are many other aspects of life that
we fantasize about, but for this writing
I'm going to leave no doubt that what
I've written on this day is true and it's about life.

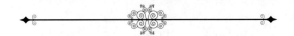

I WAS WATCHING THE NEWS

I was watching the news this morning as I sat there thinking. Robin Roberts came across the screen and said, "A young talented athlete of African descent had been shot and killed by a police officer or two." As he lay wounded, the EMT came; they treated the police officers first while the young man was handcuffed, lying in his own blood. The reports said, "After fifteen minutes of lying there wounded, dying in his own blood, his life could have been saved, 'cause all his friends wanted to help, but the other police officers said, 'Stay away.'" As they stood there watching this football star, lying in his own blood, dying, there was nothing they could do but stand there because the police officers told them to stay away.

Now comes the real truth. What did he do? From what I could tell, he did nothing to them. He was following the orders as he was given. He parked in a fire lane; that's all you need to do. He complied, and what happened? He died in the end. I was watching the news.

I was watching the news in total dismay. When are we going to learn, my friends (cops included), that you don't always have to reach and shoot. Then you want to say, "I'm sorry, I didn't mean it," but the young man is gone, he's dead, and he was lying there handcuffed, lying in his blood, and he died along the way. I was watching the news.

I was watching the news and his family was brave too. They let the world know that their son was deceased. He put family first. He believed in family from the deepest part of his heart. He went out and put a tattoo on his body that said, "Family first." I admire this young man for what he stood for and for what he believed in. It's a sad day in America that another young man has died in a senseless reaction of a police officer or two. It's sad, it's sad, it's sad. I was watching the news.

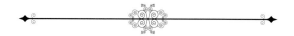

LIFE THROWS US A CURVE

Just when we think we have everything done,
Just when we know we have no worries at all,
Just when we begin to pick up the pieces and live again,
life throws us a curve.

When we come out of despair full of joy,
Full of happiness and we can see
as far as our eyes can see,
sometimes life throws us a curve.

Life throws us a curve not because it wants to
but because that's life sometimes.
Life is like a fast ball,
you blink your eyes and it's gone.
Sometimes, life is like a slow ball,
will not go by fast enough.

Sometimes, we might throw a strike
and sometimes we throw a ball,
but through it all,
life throws us a curve.

When life throws us a curve,
we take it with a smile,
we don't run and hide.
If we do, we only run for a little while . . .
but that's not the answer.

We don't run away,
we say, "Come on life, we're ready,
throw us a curve."

I may not swing at any particular pitch,
but don't be surprised if I don't hit the next curve,
but as life would have it,
it is what it is . . .
When life throws us a curve, we stand up
and we stand tall.
We raise our heads,
we dry our tears,
we clear our heads,
we put on our thinking cap and we think
positive and we say to life . . .
"Bring it on, bring it on, bring it on . . ."
because we know we're going to beat this.

Life throws us a curve,
but in the end,
it's all good that's why we call it life.
We stand up and we stand tall,
but through it all,
life throws us
a curve just like a ball.

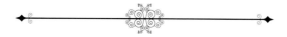

LIFE

Life has many, many meanings, and it all depends on how you see life; let's take life for the sense of the word. Life is living and life is enjoying the good things that we do. Having fun every day or two, planning a vacation, making a phone call or two, or just getting together with you know who—that's life.

Full of fun. Never, never, never on the run, but just full of fun—that's life. Life means living. It means loving someone that you care for and enjoying someone that you have the desire to be with and someone you love. Life means being with family, getting up in the morning, looking at the sun, and feeling the sun rays upon your body, or it could be just standing out in the rain like a bird with your arms extended and letting the rain touch your body gently. Life . . . Life, as precious as it can be, we want to live it to the fullest. For me, life is enjoying what God gave both you and me. Sometimes we don't understand what the Maker is thinking or what He is doing, but we know that's life.

There will be times when we're frustrated with the way things are going in life. It could be on the job, it could be family, it could be friends, it could be someone that you have an interest in, or it could be things going wrong on a given day, but we don't give up, that's what we say. We stand tall and we deal with life's woes because we know that it's life.

Life is being able to breathe God's fresh air, to explore all the things that are out there, never living in one narrow spot, for the world that God created is a huge parking lot. Never give in to what you believe in. Stand firm, that's what I say, because it's life.

Life is to love a man. Life is to love a beautiful, warm, loving, caring, and attractive woman who is your mate and who will be there regardless. That's life.

Life I must enjoy because I have no other choice, for God gave it to me and God can take it away. I must enjoy this day; no matter which way, I must enjoy this day. I know God gives and I know God takes away, but my God gives us this day and each day. Then we rise and we see the sunshine.

I want you to know, as you read this, life is wonderful no matter what! No matter the time of the day, the time of the hour, or the time of night, it is still life.

Enjoy life, raise that head up, stick that chest out, walk like a million-dollar man or woman, look up to the sky, and say, "God, You gave me this day. You gave me this life. I'm going to live it to the fullest. I love life. I'm thankful for life. Thank You, God, because You are life."

WE HAVE ALL DONE SOMETHING WRONG

We were born into this world not knowing whether we would survive the first few minutes or whether we would live a full life. However, that is determined; we have all done something wrong. We cannot judge our neighbors, friends, brothers, sisters, or even strangers. For within all of us, we have done something wrong. Sometimes we want to project that we are the perfect angel, when in fact, we know that we have all done something wrong. We ask for forgiveness because we are not perfect. For some, it is a struggle to live the golden rule. We ask God Almighty to forgive us and to give us strength so that we may become stronger, but in the end, we have all done something wrong. No matter how we look at it, no matter how we twist it, for some it might be a square, for others a rectangle, and for others a revolving door. We all are trying to figure out in this big old world what's right and what's wrong. No matter how life ends, we have all done something wrong. At the end of the day, we can say "Lord, forgive us because we know that you are with us no matter which way we go." But I am not going to fool myself anymore by trying to forget that I have never done anything wrong. I want all of you to know that you too are human just like me, and I can look you in your eyes and say to you, as I have said to myself, "We have all done something wrong."

FLAVOR OF THE ROSE

The flavor of the rose is an interesting story. It is about a beautiful person that cannot make up their mind on the color of the rose. It has been said, they are as sweet as they can be, they have a sense of humor that is out of this world, and they are very lovable. The flavor of the rose was originally thought of as white. As the rose grew to maturity, it became a beautiful brown rose. Once the two hearts came together, it was a majestic rose. So the question becomes "What is the flavor of the rose?"

The flavor of the rose is like a diamond. It shines like no other rose in the world. The flavor has a beautiful smile and laughter that would make the old turn new.

The flavor of the rose is like glitter and gold. There is no other like the flavor of the rose. She was warm, lovable, and very attractive. That was the true color of the rose.

It was called the flavor of the rose because people in the world didn't understand why she decided that the color of the rose didn't matter—white, pink, or red, it did not matter. She had her flavor and now the question is, what was the flavor of the rose?

As you read this, I hope that you can envision a beautiful rose as it spreads love all over the world and then comes back full circle to the flavor of the rose. As the story goes, she was really the flavor of the rose. She loved what she loved, and she cared for what she cared for. She didn't mind speaking up for what was right and for what was wrong. She found a light brown rose, and when they came together, it was a majestic rose. It was a rose that she could say to all of you, "Do you know the flavor of the rose?" And now you have it, the flavor of the rose. They lived a long and happy life together as one flavor and as one rose. To my friend, you now have the flavor and the rose too.

MY BODY

My body is what it is. In younger years it was strong; I had muscles that I could show. I didn't know much about foot moves unless I was playing on the football field. On the dance floor, man, I was a flop, and today I'm not much better. That's my body. With foot aches and pains, sometimes it's hard to move. Sometimes it just does not want to get in gear. But you know, that's my body. It has been a good body, it's had a lot of fun, and it's seen a lot of things; it has had a few bumps and a few lumps, but it came out all right. Someday, I don't know where my body may end up.

Now they tell me I should look at the healthy part of my mind to create a healthy part of my body. Some call it soul and mind; I call it just getting old.

Whatever the case may be, I have to go with the flow because I have a heavy load. I look forward to the day many, many years from now as this story will be told. Some will look back and read my writings, and they will try to digest what I was thinking and what I was not, but in the end, there is a fold, and in this case it's my body as it's being told.

DULCY

There is a lady that we call Dulcy. Her name means sweetness. She is really sweet. Sweetness always strolled in the office dressed to kill. If you didn't know any better, you would think that she comes from royalty.

She is one of the sweetest people you could ever meet on God's earth. She has class. She drives a 300Z convertible. Even in her golden age, she can turn heads. She sports "C Me Fly 2" on her car tag. Sweetness is her name.

She reminds me of success and sweetness. Sweetness in her smile, sweetness in her voice, sweetness in the way she styles her hair, sweetness in the way she walked, sweetness in the way she talked, and sweetness in all the other things that one. Sweetness is her name.

As we travel this life, I hope and pray that all of us get a chance to touch and know someone that has the true meaning of sweetness. Someone that you will know years from now that will make you smile. We called her sweetness. Sweetness is her name. I can't help but love her. Sweetness, sweetness, and sweetness is her name.

WE HAVE ALL BEEN THERE

When we think everything is going fine and something happens. Maybe that we have no money, bills due, family calling and asking for a favor or two, car that broke down—it could be anything; we have all been there. Sitting at home, worried to death whether the tow man is coming for the car, if the rent-to-own people are coming for the TV, bedroom suite, washer and dryer, or refrigerator—we have all been there.

Wanting to go out with nothing to wear, having to roll pennies just to feed the kids—we have all been there. When we think that we are secure in our job and everything is going fine, then the boss comes in and says, "We have to lay some of you off today." We don't know what to do or which way to turn because we were not making enough to save a dime. Now the rent's going to come due and the car payment too. You don't know what to do, but we have been there.

Crying our tears out, walking the floor, calling friends, relatives, and maybe the preacher too, and hating to ask for a dollar or two, but we have all been there too.

We have all been there and we do not know what to do or whom to ask for a favor or two, but we know that we have all been there too. We reach from our inner strength but we still have to ask ourselves that million-dollar question: "What am I going to do?" In the end, all we can say is "we have been there too."

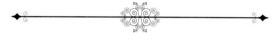

ENJOY

Life can be so wonderful sometimes and all we can say is enjoy. Life can be difficult and all we can say is enjoy. No matter how we look at life, whether we are going up the highway, down the highway, down the mountains, or a straightaway playing with the curves—life . . . enjoy.

Life will always have ups and downs. You will have folks who will tell you what to do but have no clue, and they don't want to hear that. So I say, "Enjoy life, enjoy."

There will be days that you just don't want to get up, days that you are frustrated for whatever reason, days where the mind plays tricks on you, days when the brain is sending so many signals in every which way but the right way. Enjoy life.

Enjoy life to the fullest no matter how it comes at you because, if you have any relationship with God, you will enjoy that second, that minute, that hour, that day, and that night because joy comes in the morning, late at night, and anytime in between when you have a relationship with your God.

Life enjoy, enjoy, enjoy. When it's all over with and you can't do anymore. Just when the body says no more, just look back on all the things that you were able to do and reflect back on things that you just could not finish.

At the end of the day, no matter which way you go, no matter which way the mood may swing, no matter which way the thoughts may linger, in the end, enjoy, enjoy, enjoy.

WE LIVE

We live to love, to smile, to share, to care—we live. We live to wake up in the morning. We live to have kids. We live to share the life of grandkids. We live to work. We live to make money. We live, we live.

We live to love others. We live to care for others. We live to have the greatest joys in the world and that is to love our God; we live. We live to have a relationship with God because we know that all things come through Him. We live for His teachings, we live for His words, we live to do the things that He would want us to do, but we live.

We live to have fun. We know that life will bring us sadness, despair, tears, pain, joy, and hopefully much happiness, but we live. We live to see the beauty of God's creation. We live for the four seasons: spring, summer, fall, and winter, but we live. We live to see the trees change colors, the beauty of God's creation. In the summer season, the trees create their leaves, and in the fall they change colors and they fall. In the winter, all of God's creation of trees becomes naked and in the spring, the rain brings back to life the trees and the leaves. We live for the seasons. We may complain about spring, summer, fall, and winter, but we live, we live and we live.

DON'T READ INTO THINGS

We have a conversation about this and that. Sometimes it seems that we have reached a compromise, sometimes it seems that there may be a little confusion, but sometimes it is crystal clear; but don't read anything into that.

Sometimes we listen but not with a full ear. Sometimes we see but not with clear eyes. Sometimes we feel but not with true feelings. Sometimes we think but not with a clear head. But don't read anything into that.

Sometimes we read or hear a poem, see a TV clip, or hear a conversation that someone is attempting to share with us, but we didn't hear all the story; we only heard what we wanted to hear. Don't read into things. Maybe someone shared something with you, read a story or two, or have even left you out. It was not intentional, no matter what it may have been, but the bottom line is, don't read into it.

As life would have it, we're not perfect. Sometimes when we are thinking one way, our mind is running another. Sometimes when we are seeing one way, we are seeing another. Sometimes when we are hearing, we are hearing something or the other. But at the end of the day, I just say, "Don't read into things."

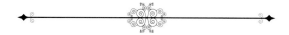

WHAT MAKES THE WORLD GO ROUND?

What makes the world go round we will never know. We all have an idea, but what really makes the world go round are the folks that are in it. There are good folks and bad, and no matter how we twist and turn it, for a lot of folks, it will still come out sad. But we must ask ourselves, what makes the world go round? There are many versions of what makes the world go round. We can talk about this and that, and I think we can all come to the conclusion that it's love.

We can talk about money because it too makes the world go round. People, sceneries, families, friends, or even loved ones can make the world go round. You can look toward the hills, the valleys, the mountains, the trees, and the animals. This is what makes the world go round.

What makes the world go round for some, they will never know, and for others, they go out and do everything they can to uplift and give a hand to fellow man or woman. This old world was created for us so that we are able to do the things that we need to do and where God intended for us to as well.

Each one of us, no matter who you are, where you are, what your status is in life, it doesn't matter. We all have something to offer, and I hope that, as you read some of my writings, by now you have come to the conclusion that there is something in all of us that makes the world go round. You have to be mindful to do what comes natural.

In the end, you too will know what makes the world go round.

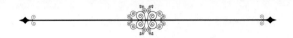

WHAT IS THIS LIFE SUPPOSED TO BE LIKE

What is this life supposed to be like? I don't know. All that I know is that I am going to make the best out of this life because I know that tomorrow is not promised. I know that the world is changing, and attitudes are changing too. Therefore, I don't know what this world is supposed to be like.

What is this world supposed to be like? A very loving and caring world. A world that no matter who we are, no matter where we came from, and no matter where we are going, we are seen as one.

Sometimes we act as if we are the only ones in this old world, but frankly, if you believe that, then you will have a rude awakening someday. What is this old world supposed to be like? I don't know, but what I do know is that I'm going to give it my best and I'm going to do everything that I know to do that's right, and with that, I believe I will be able to spread love throughout this nation.

What is this old world supposed to be like? I don't know, but I do know that I am glad to be a part of this old world and to make a contribution to it. I am proud of who I am and for those individual lives that I have touched in my life.

I don't know what this old world is supposed to be like, but I do know that, as long as I am in this old world, I will be like the sun—I shall shine. I will be like the wind that blows—you will hear me. And I will be like the snow that falls—I will take my period of hibernation and come back, so all will know that I'm still in this old world. Yet I don't know what this old world is supposed to be like, but for me it's all about you.

BAD HABIT

I have a bad habit of smoking, you see, I tried to stop and I just couldn't see. I got a bad habit of smoking, and sometimes I think it smokes me. I would love to quit, but I don't know what to do. I'm addicted to smoking just like you. I know folks would love for me to quit, but again I don't know what to do because I'm addicted just like you.

I have a bad habit of drinking too and I've tried to stop and I found myself useless. I spent all my money just for what, I don't know, but for the smell of beer and a beer belly gut. I would love to stop drinking too, but at this point in my life, I don't know what else to do!

My so-called friends all run away and say bad things about me because I love my Seagram's too. I have a bad habit of drinking and I don't know what else to do, and I'm addicted to drinking just like you.

Someday I'll hang both of these bad habits up to dry, but until then, I'll have to smoke and drink on the sly. I'm trying to fool folks, yes, I am, but I think they know that I'm addicted to both. Please help me if you can because I don't know what else to do. All I can say is "I am addicted and I need help just like you."

WHEN THIS OLD WORLD IS OVER

When this old world is over and I have lived my life and I have done everything that I thought was right and I have done a few things that I'm not pleased with, all I can say is "When this old world is over, I have lived."

When this old world is over and before I go, I hope to have a chance to look back on all the things that I didn't do, wanted to do, couldn't do, and didn't have time to do and ask myself, "Why not?"

When this old world is over, I can say well done to my friends and walk away with a smile. We know our stay here on earth is numbered, and when this old world is over, I have lived.

When this old world is over, I hope you can look back and say, "I did what my God instructed me to do. I did all the things that I wanted to. I spoke up for the less fortunate, gave away some of my most precious belongings, and helped many others along the way too." I hope that, when this old world is over, I can be as proud as you because I know I have tried my darnest to make a difference in me, you, and all the others too. When this old world is over, I will go out with a smile. Thank you, Lord; thank you, Lord; just plain old thank you because I have lived.

THIS COULD BE YOU

When you think everything is all right and something goes wrong, this could be you. When you think you have all your bills laid out to pay and you use a debit card, you find that your accounts have been debited twice, and now your checks are beginning to bounce, this could be you.

When you have had a faithful car, washer, dryer, or something that has served you well, then all of a sudden it goes haywire or it breaks and now you don't know what to do, this could be you.

When you have planned everything down to the last detail, you know what you want to do, how you are going to do it, and how you are going to carry it off, and then something goes wrong, this could be you.

When you have worked all your life and have raised your kids and you think that you can settle down and enjoy living on a fixed income, you get a phone call from your kids or grandkids that say "I need this," and now all of a sudden you must help! You pull your money from every account in the world to help. This could be you.

When you go to work every day and do an honest day's work for an honest day's pay and things begin to unravel in the office with company personalities and politics, then all of a sudden nothing seems to be right. You leave work, not knowing what to do, what to say, or what to expect. This could be you.

When we know that everything is great and happiness is everywhere, planning ahead for a summer vacation or a nice cruise, and then all of a sudden something unusual happens too, this could be you.

When you read this writing and you find that it touches you too, just say to yourself, this could be you too!

Love

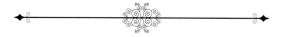

LOVE

Love is an expression of the heart because, without the heart, there could be no love, for the heart pumps all the blood throughout the body and it registers dead center to the brain.

Love. Without the heart, there is no love. It is an imaginary feeling of true disbelief. The heart is what really makes a person love.

Love is more than an expression. Sometimes it is a connection of the soul, of the mind, of the body. It is a connection that some folks never ever experience, but love of the heart is an exception.

Love can make a person do things they say that they would never do, and love will make a person say things they would never say. Love can drive you crazy, but what we look for in love is one that's warming, loving, or caring and one that has compassion too where we can communicate the true meaning of the word love.

Love is like no other. It is a feeling that you know when two hearts meet and two hands touch; when the lips lock together and the sensation that comes over our bodies, minds, souls, and hearts. They let you know that it's love. Love is when you miss someone so dearly, but the heart tells you yes, no matter what, it will be okay and it's okay to miss someone that you love. It's okay to think about someone that you love. Love is a universal word that, if it is nurtured to its fullest potential, we as human beings will experience a feeling never ever felt before.

Love is the joining of the universe mentally, spiritually, and devotionally the hearts, the minds, and the souls. Love is what we all as human beings live for. Love.

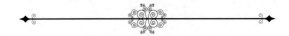

I TRIED, BUT YOU WOULDN'T LET ME

I tried, but you wouldn't let me love you. You wouldn't let me give you all the beautiful things in the world that there is to give. I tried to text you, call you, caress you, love you with every ounce in my body, but you wouldn't let me.

I tried, but you wouldn't let me, and I wouldn't give up because I knew somewhere, somehow, that I had to get through to you. I don't know what it is, but I do know it's something—something that you're holding back, something that you're not telling, or something that happened to you and you're not ready to say, but I tried and you wouldn't let me.

I tried, but you wouldn't let me love you the way I wanted to, but I didn't give up because I can feel the love that you have in your heart. I know that you're distant, but it's not because of something that I did; maybe it was something that I said or something that was done to you before me, or just maybe you had a bad relation, one or two. I really don't know. I know I still love you, and I'll say it again, I tried, but you wouldn't let me.

I tried, but you wouldn't let me, but I wouldn't give up. I see something in those beautiful brown eyes. I see something in your soul that's standing, there reaching and asking, "Please touch me." I see with such intensity that there is a lovely, sweet, warm, caring person that's inside of that shell that says, "I love you, but I'm not giving up on you this day, tomorrow, or next year." I tried, but you wouldn't let me.

I tried, but you wouldn't let me love you. You wouldn't let me love you, but I know deep down in my heart that love won't let me run away. I know what I see, what I hear, what I feel. I'm going to be patient, for some day you will let me and then I can say, "I tried and you let me," and when you do, I will love you, love you, love you. I tried and you finally let me. With love, just me.

BE THERE FOR ME AND I'LL BE THERE FOR YOU

Be there for me and I'll be there for you—it's the only way to go. When we decided to love one another, we decided to be one. I know how to be there for you at night when you're in pain, at night when you can't sleep, at night when you want to snuggle, or during the day when you have troubles, or when you're laughing, or when you're talking, or when you have an opinion or two. I know how to be there for you. Be there for me because I'll be there for you. I'll be there when you want me. I'll be there to hold you, to touch you, to call your name, to say all those sweet things I know you like to hear that make you feel like a real woman. I know how to be there for you.

You've been there for me on more than one occasion. You listen patiently; you smiled with such deep passion. You bring that sparkle to my eyes, the dimples in my smile; you've been there for me. I see things that I've never seen before and I've felt things that I've never felt, and I know the quietness of your posture does not mean you don't agree; it does not mean you don't care. You have a silent way of saying "I'll be there." I'll never take that away from you because I know it's true, and I thank you for loving me and I thank you for being there. Be there for me and I'll be there for you.

Be there for me and I'll be there for you until the end because we're together as one. We cannot be separated no matter how they pull us, no matter how they try. No matter, when day turns into darkness and darkness turns into daylight. No matter, if the rain comes, the hail comes, the wind comes, it does not matter. I'll be there for you and you'll be there for me.

They can't stop a love like ours, because they are on the outside. "Jealous" is what we say to all of those. Take a page from us and learn to say, "Be there for me and I'll be there for you." And I will always be there for you.

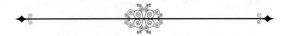

LOVE IS BLINDING

Love is blinding, that's what they say. I'm not sure if I can see along the way. She comes with a beautiful smile and a fine body too, and all of a sudden I'm taken in by you-know-who. "Love is blinding" is what they say. I'm not sure if I can see along the way. She says, all the sweet things you want to hear. She has a gentle touch that will last for years. Her love is unbeatable; if you want to measure it, I can't. I had nothing like this until she came along. They tell me that love is blinding and I can't see.

"Love is blinding" is what they say, but what a love I found along the way. I think about her all the time no matter where I am, no matter what I'm doing—they tell me love is blinding.

Love is blinding when you can't see, but that's all right too because it's for both you and me. I give my all and so does she. We dance, we smile, we talk, we chitchat, we exchange ideas, we plan, we do crazy things in the spur of the moment, and we let it flow no matter which way it goes. So they say, love is blinding, so I guess it is. But let me say again: "Love is blinding because of you and me." I can't see, she can't see, so I guess they're right.

Love is blinding and neither one of us can see. Love is blinding.

A GOOD MAN SHOULD SEE

A good man should see the beauty of a woman. Her smile, her passion, and all the hot desires in the heart of a real woman. A good man should see the beauty in her walk, the beauty in her talk, the beauty in the style of clothes she wears—the beauty of a real woman, a good man should see.

Don't be fooled by a fast talker, fancy dresser, or fast money. A real woman should not see. A good man should see all the things that a good woman needs whether it be a hug, a kiss, a simple hello, or a small task or two; a good man should see, and if you love her as you say you do, you will be able to see the beauty of a real woman. She doesn't have to tell you what she needs or what she wants, what she desires, or any other thing—a good man should see.

A good man understands a woman's joy. He understands her pain. He understands what she needs, when she needs it, and what she wants when she wants it, and what she dreams for all her life is for two hearts to become one.

A good man should see that as he travels the highway, he'll think of me. As he goes off to work to do a day's job, he'll think of me. When he is riding down the highway with nothing to see, he'll think of me. When he passes the mall and wonders what thing he could buy for his baby, he'll think of me. Break time, lunch time, and the time in between, he'll think of me. If he loves me the way he says he does, he'll think of me. That's what a good man should do and see.

A good man is hard to come by and not like those who are fast talkers and slick dressers and have fast money and are just trying to hit and run—that's not for a good woman to ever see. So I say to you, a good man should see the beauty, warmth, love, passion, desire, fire, need, and all things in between that makes a good man want to see. Those are some qualities that you have that a good man should always see.

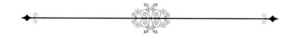

I FELL DEEPLY IN LOVE WITH THEE

I fell deeply in love with thee because I could see, I could see me, I could see you, and I could see us. I knew from the start that I fell in love with thee.

Loneliness can make the heart grow fonder, they say, but when two hearts meet, they never stray. The love that we have shall never go away because I know I fell in love with thee.

I know you think of me in the wee hours of the morning, midday, and sometimes late in the evenings as you travel on your way. You feel me, you sense me, and you know I'm there because you know I truly care. I fell in love with thee.

Love is wonderful, love is great, love has its twists and turns, but that's okay because love is a wonderful thing. I want you to know today, tomorrow, tonight—I fell in love with thee.

I LOVE YOU

I love you, darling, and I dream about you every day and every night that I lay my head down to sleep. Of course I pray to the good Lord that he continue to keep us together and our lives continue to spread and grow like no other. I love you darling because you have that warm sense about you that makes my heart glow. No matter how low I get, I will always know that your love is there for me.

I love you, darling, because I think about all the things that we have done together, things that we have shared together, things that we have planned together, and things that we still dream of doing together, and most importantly I love you for the way that you treat me and respect me.

I love you like no other man will ever love you. I will show what it means to have someone that is near you and what it means to have someone that will stand by you no matter what. I love you because the world is filled with folks who have never ever experienced the real meaning of love.

The real meaning of love is to hold you at night, caress your body like no other, and give you the sense of security that you have never ever felt. I look into your eyes and softly say to you, "I love you, I love you, I love you." And when it's time to retire at night, we give each other a hug, a kiss, and an "I love you and good night." That is what real love is all about. Always letting you know that you are loved and cared about more than anything in this world.

I love you because, when I am not around you, I can still feel the love that flows between the two of us. I can feel you touching my heart, body, mind, and soul. I can feel you as though you are sitting next to me and you are saying those words that everybody loves to hear: "I love you, dear." And I love you more than anything in the world.

I love you, I love you, and I love you. The word *love*, when it is acted upon from the deepest part of a person's heart, will always give a warm feeling, and you know that it is love like no other.

I love you, darling. I will never let anyone or anybody make you believe otherwise. I am proud to be your man, your friend, your lover, your soul mate, or the person that you know will always be there for you. With love, my dear.

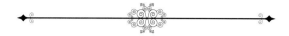

I LOVE YOU FOR WHO YOU ARE

I love you, darling, for who you are and for what you could be. I have searched the world over and I found you. Now is the time for you to be the woman that you want to be. Don't let life situations throw you back, because you have the potential to fight back. That's why I love you for who you are.

I love you for who you are because you are someone special. You are special because God made you special. You have evolved into a beautiful woman as you continue to travel life's highway. I want you to always be surrounded by the love of who you are and who you are with. You are someone special.

I love you for who you are and for not who you once were or where you came from or what you may have done before we met. I love you for who you are today and for who you will become tomorrow, and what I see is an independent African woman that has the genes of an African queen. I love you for who you are.

We are brought into this world, not knowing what's right or what's wrong. We are brought into this world to love, not to hate, not to make waste, to understand, and to do crazy things without a plan, but as we grew, we became young men and young women. God stepped into our lives and because of that, I can say, "I love you for who you are."

To some, you may not mean anything, but to me you mean everything. Don't look back on life, because it is gone. You can't take back yesterday, last year, or before, but we look forward to tomorrow and we always want love along the way. When you find it my love, don't lose it, don't let it run away from you. I love you for who you are.

I love you for who you are because you are trying every day of your life to be a better person. I love you because you see there is a tomorrow. I love you because you are no longer in despair. I love you because you listen. I love you because you offer your opinion. I love you not for what you can do, but I love you for what you can be. So always know that you are loved and you're special in many ways. Don't let anyone steal your joy, and don't let anyone turn you backward; go forward, my love, and do the things that are good and make those that you love proud to say, "I love you for who you have become."

I FELL IN LOVE

Sometimes we look for things and we find what we don't want to find, and despite everything, I fell in love a time or two. Multiply that by how many and I will never tell you. They were not all bad. I gave it my best. I fell in love. I fell in love because of my heart; sometimes it was because of my mind, and sometimes it was lust. But either way, good or bad, I fell in love.

I fell in love because love is blinding. Sometimes we see things that we don't see. Sometimes we hear what we don't want to hear, and we still fall in love.

Falling in love is not the worst thing in the world. Love can be fun, love can be happiness, love can be pure joy, and other times love can be a pain that makes you cry. Love can make you ache, and you feel all torn up inside, but as time goes by, the heart heals and so does the mind. We'll look back many years from now and we'll say I fell in love once upon a time.

Not all loves are going to be great. Some are going to have so much passion that we can't wait. We put off doing things that we need to do because we feel that passion is waiting for you. Sometimes we call it hot love, sometimes we call it the real stuff, sometimes we don't call it anything, but we call it love at least. That's what some would say. Either way, as we go through this life, most of us can say, "I fell in love once upon a time." Once upon a time I was happy as I could be and there were times that even a tear couldn't protect me. But when it's all said and done, we'll smile, laugh, talk, and chitchat. Who knows, we might add a line or two, but we can all say, "We fell in love a time or two. Multiply that by how many and I will never tell you."

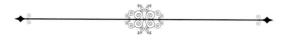

THE WOMAN WHO STOLE MY HEART

I fell in love with you as deeply as it could be. I fell in love with you because I knew you were the woman for me. You are the woman who stole my heart. You're the woman who stole my heart and you ran away, but you came back the same day. You love me dearly because I can see. For within you, I do see myself. From the first day until now, I still see that lovely smile. I know time will reveal that you were the woman who stole my heart.

I think about you as often as can be and I can only imagine the sweet sound of how intimacy would be. You are such a beautiful person with such a beautiful smile, and I know you want this love to be your last love of all. You are the woman who stole my heart.

The first time I laid eyes on you, I knew you were for me, I knew you were like a diamond in the rough that needed some smoothing, but I knew you were in love with me. I put my best foot forward, I opened my heart, and I gave you all the love that one man could give because you are the woman who stole my heart.

I smile, I dream, I imagine, and I think about the woman who stole my heart. She must be part of the African queen.

When it's all said and done, you will have time to reflect back upon this love and you too can say those words "You are the man who stole my heart." I took it as gently as could be. I nurtured it, I cared for it, and I let you know that it was love to be. I never ran away with your heart. I just loved you because you loved me and there was no way that I could run away, but I knew I could steal your heart. Those eyes of yours just didn't know what I could see, but as time flew by, I knew it was you and me. I had no doubts, none at all. Sometimes I may have wandered left and right, but I knew it was you and me.

You are that lady as beautiful as can be with those beautiful eyes only meant for a queen bee. You are that lady no matter how you look at it, no matter how you think about it, no matter how you feel, and not to mention how wonderful and loving the moment of the thrill.

I can say to you like you can say to me, "I'm the man who stole your heart and you are the woman who stole mine too." I love you. You be sweet and always remember me because you are that woman who stole my heart.

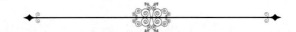

YOU ASK CRAZY THINGS OF ME

You ask crazy things of me and that's okay too because it's you. I don't mind jumping through hoops. I don't mind dancing around. I don't mind doing the impossible because you ask crazy things of me.

I gave you a new life and exposed you to some new things. I gave you a chance to see the world in a different light with me. Surprised and amazed you were, but again that's okay because you ask crazy things of me.

Crazy things are fun to you. Just understand it's not all about you. Your smile, your laugh, your cry, just to name a few. Occasionally I may do something crazy too, but our craziness is not so crazy and we never do anything to hurt each other, even though you might ask crazy things of me. Love is fun and love is happiness. I don't mind you asking crazy things of me.

I CAN SEE

I can see looking into your eyes, the beauty of your soul, the beauty of your heart, and the beauty of your mind because I can see. I can see the roughness in your thought process. I can see the smoothness in your heart. I can see the determination of the day gone by, and I can see the passion as it rolls off of your beautiful thigh. I can see.

I can see the world through you. I can see when the clouds are cloudy, I can see when the rain is raining, I can see when the sun is shining, and I can see when you see because I can see.

I can see like no other. I can see, I can feel, I can touch, I can hear, I can listen, and I can see. I can see looking into your eyes like no other man has ever seen, and on this day, I don't think there is a man who can see the beauty in you but me.

I want you to know, no matter where you go, no matter what you do in life, I will always be within you. I will always be in your heart. I will always be in your mind. And I will always be in your soul and your thoughts because I can see, and I can see the beauty of you and me.

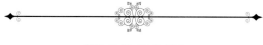

I'M DONE

I gave you everything that you have asked for, including my last dollar, and you are still not satisfied. I'm done. I have listened to your stories and then some, and that's not enough. I'm done.

You ask for a new car and you get it; a new house filled with furniture and you get it; an expense account and you get it; and that's not enough. I'm done.

I wait on you hand and foot, iron your clothes, cook you meals, make sure the house is clean, and never ask where you have been when you come home, and that's not enough. I'm done.

You miss my birthdays, anniversaries, and holidays, and I say nothing, but that's not enough. I'm done.

Your bills are due and you have no money and I pay them. You need clothes and I buy them. You run out of money and I give you mine, and that's not enough. I'm done.

I plan yearly vacations, mini vacations, and weekend getaways, and you promise me that you will be there for all of them, and you don't show. That's not good enough. I'm done.

You would have me believe that you love me, you care for me, and you miss me. You say, there's no one else like me and that I am the diamond in your eyes; but you always find an excuse of some sort, and I believe any excuse that you give me. But that's not good enough. I'm done.

I know what you just read; there is a line in there for you too. We have all done things to try to satisfy somebody, and when we finally reach that point of no return, we have to say to that person, "That's not good enough." I'm done.

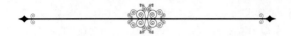

I'M SMOKING AND I'M GRILLING

I'm smoking and I'm grilling it really tastes good. Folks are stopping by wanting a piece of this and a piece of pie. I'm smoking and I'm grilling, and I'm as happy as I can be because I know on this day, there are many folks like me. We're out having fun and we're out flipping and grilling 'cause I know it is, umm, good.

Flipping and grilling is what we all like to do sometimes. It may come the first of the year, July 4, or in the middle of the week. If the urge hits you, just remember, there's nothing wrong with flipping and grilling. I love flipping and grilling and I love to chow down, so I want folks to know try it sometimes, you might like it. Umm, it smells good, folks are stopping by, but I want you to know that I'm enjoying myself and I love it when I'm flipping and grilling. I love it when I can flip it and grill it, just flipping and just grilling.

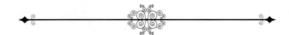

THE LADY OF MY DREAMS

The lady of my dreams has come and gone. But to me I can tell you that she is like a princess. It is equal to a queen—the lady of my dreams.

The lady of my dreams is beautiful. She is tall and very attractive with a nice body. She has brown eyes, a sense of humor out of this world, a beautiful smile, and jet-black hair—the lady of my dreams.

The lady of my dreams can only truly be a queen, not a princess. What was I thinking? The bloodline for a queen, and especially an African queen, is of such that it would warm the heart, mind, soul, toes, and eyes—every part of the human body. That's my dream for my African queen. She is definitely the lady of my dreams.

Now she has grown older and her hair is sprinkled with beautiful gray. She is still the lady of my dreams. Those nice, fine brown legs are showing the beauty of age. She is still the lady of my dreams. Her smile has not changed. You can tell through her eyes that she has been around—the lady of my dreams.

The lady of my dreams can still make me smile and reads my mind to tell me what I am thinking. She corrects me when I am wrong, she compliments me when I am right, and she is there to support me in every aspect of my life. That's the lady of my dreams.

The lady of my dreams—when I wake up, I find that she is the lady that I have been with for so many wonderful years. That's the lady of my dreams.

I have named her Meme. She is mine and she is the lady of my dreams. I hope everyone can say, read, think, dream, and most importantly visualize the lady of your dreams. Mine is Meme.

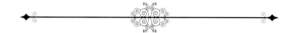

THE WOMAN IN RED

Wow! It was the ultimate surprise
to see a woman in red—it caused the heart to flow,
the heart to beat and the legs to become weak.
The woman in red.

Wow! She allowed the dream to become the dreamer,
the imaginer to imagine,
and the thoughts to become written words.
The woman in red.

Wow! Just to see the beauty of red lipstick upon her
lips made me think of strawberries dipped in chocolate.
The woman in red.

Wow! That red dress worn with a sweater,
with red painted nails and red heels.
Again, those beautiful lips covered in red.

It's like a dream come true, but all I could
do is compliment her.
She has all the curves a man likes.
The woman in red.

She is spoken for and my only dream for her
is to be blessed.
Maybe another time, another place—
I'll see her again and say to myself,
"Why couldn't she be mine?"
Maybe in the next life . . .

Wow! The woman in red.
Live on because God blessed you.
The woman in red. My love, my dreams.
The woman in red.

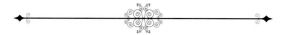

MAKE ME SMILE

Make me smile when I look into your beautiful eyes.

Make me smile when you touch me.

Make me smile when you whisper sweet things to me.

Make me smile when you make me proud.

Make me smile when I hear your voice.

Make me smile when I dream about you.

Make me smile when we are together.

Make me smile knowing that you love

me with all your heart.

Make me smile when all else fails.

Make me smile just knowing we are together.

Make me smile when you smile.

Make me smile baby and make me proud

to love the greatest person in the world.

Make me smile!

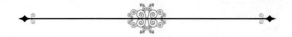

WAITING FOR THE RIGHT MAN

I'm waiting for the right man to come my way. I'm waiting for the right man to come my way, and when he does, I will be prepared to show him my way. He has to be someone with a nice sense of humor and a pleasant personality and who is fun, loving, caring, and passionate. I'm waiting for the right man to come.

I'm waiting for the right man to come, and he must be a God-fearing man. A man that understands what we have to do, all the things that the Good Book teaches you. We must live by the golden rules without any exceptions. I'm waiting for the right man to come.

I'm waiting for the right man to come because I know my God is going to send him my way. I will be warm, open, responsive, respectable, and very conscious of all the things in between. I'm waiting for a good man to come.

I'm waiting for a good man to come because a good man is waiting for a good woman to come. We are living in an age where a good man is hard to come by and a good man just does not want to treat a good woman right. When a woman is independent and trying to do all the right things and make a relationship work, the average man wants to play the field. I'm not interested in that! I'm interested in a God-fearing man that believes in doing what's right and not what's wrong.

I'm waiting for a good man to come because the time is right. I have matured in my ways and thinking. I know what I am looking for and the standards that he must meet. I'm not overbearing; I'm just independent, and I know that I am not impossible to be with or to work with. I am waiting for a good man to come.

I'm waiting for a good man to come because I am full of love, joy, and happiness. I have an inspiration within me that will make a good man glow. I know I can stand the test and I'm ready. So if there are any good men out there, just let me know. I'm waiting for a good man to come. In the same breath, I know a good man is waiting for a good woman, and I'm proud to say to any man that I am a good woman looking for a good man to come my way.

I LOVED THAT MAN

I loved that man more than anything in the world. I have gone above and beyond for his love. I love that man because of who he is and the way he treats me. I will spend my last dime on him and run my credit card to the max. I would work three jobs. I would do whatever he asked of me because I loved that man.

There are days that I am floating on cloud nine with nowhere to go but to think about him, waiting patiently for him to come through the door so I can say, "I love you."

I loved that man because of his smile, his touch, his way of thinking, and the way he words things. They all fill me with love. I loved that man.

I loved that man even when he didn't love me. I didn't realize that he didn't love me until it was too late. I was blindsided because I loved that man. Friends would tell me things and my relatives too; but I couldn't believe it because I loved that man.

One day I was walking in the mall, minding my own business, and I heard a voice say "Hello, how are you?" from out of nowhere. I responded, "I am fine." The man said, "You look like you have been beat down."

At that point, all I could do was try to raise my head, and when I did, I said, "Oh my God." That was the beginning of a new life for me. I began to realize on that day that the love that I had for the man I thought loved me was about to leave my heart for another man.

He said, "Why don't we sit down and have a glass of tea and just talk." At first, I was reluctant. Then I gave in. From that day until now, I can say to you I got a real man and he truly loves me.

He has shown me what it's like to be loved. He has included me into all the things that we do. I can say to you I got a real man and I love that man.

I want you to know that you too can find new love. You never know when love is going to hit you. It hit me in the mall with a nice glass of tea. Today, I want everyone to know that I got a real man. I love that man. Soon he shall be my husband and I his wife. I got a real man and he loves me. I love that man.

Family and Friends

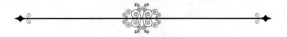

SHE LOST A DAUGHTER

She lost a daughter that she loved so very much. She went through trial and tribulations with her. Sometimes a mother's love isn't enough when there is a substance out there that takes control of the body, the mind, the soul and makes you crave for more. She lost a daughter.

She lost a daughter, and it hurt so much. She did as a mother all she could do by protecting her, looking after here, and visiting her too, but in the end, that wasn't enough. She lost a daughter.

She lost a daughter and she weeps and she weeps. She thinks about all the fun that they had together when she was a little kid, watching her grow up to become a teenager and then to become a mother. She thinks about all the things she said and things that she did not have a chance to say, but she lost a daughter.

She loved her daughter like no other, and she prayed every day that she would win the battle, but sometimes the battle got hard. But a mother's love caused her to stick by her daughter. She loved her so much, but in the end, a mother's love wasn't enough.

She lost a daughter that reminded her of laughter, happiness, and fun. Just when time seems to just run, run, and run. She lost a daughter that she loved so very much.

She lost a daughter that she loves so much that she would have traded places to see her daughter live a full life and watch her grandchildren grow up, but God knew best and a mother's love wasn't enough.

She thinks about her daughter like all the other children she bore. No parent ever wants to think that their child should go first. She did all that she could do, and she couldn't do anymore, and she placed the daughter that she loved so much in the hands of the Lord.

Her daughter fought a long battle, and they all thought the battle had been won, but in the end . . . a mother's love wasn't enough.

She just left this world so suddenly and the hurt of her passing is still fresh in her mother's mind, heart and soul. But Mom knows God knows best. She lost a daughter.

She lost a daughter and despite her fight, she left a legacy of love, happiness, and compassion for others. It wasn't always a fight to live nor was it a fight to die, but it was a fight to stay away from that substance that has taken so many lives. She lost a daughter.

In the end, there are many of you who have lost a daughter, son, niece, nephew, brother, mother, father, friend, relative, or a stranger to a substance that has no end.

I want the world to know: don't give up and don't give in, and surround your loved ones with love the best that you can!

In the end, when you have done all that you can do, just put your loved ones in the hands of the Lord because you know He will fight that battle to the end. She lost a daughter.

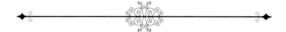

MOM IS NOT GONE

Mom is not gone.
She has gone home to God's kingdom.
The kingdom in the sky
where Mom shall never fear, never cry,
Never have another pain;
That's the kingdom in the sky.

Mom is not gone.
She lives on in the hearts, minds, and souls
Of all those she touched, helped,
or gave a helping hand to . . . that's still untold.
Her legacy of love still lives on.

Mom is not gone.
She had gone on to that wonderful,
peaceful, and joyful place God calls home.
She is not gone.

Mom lives on.
Her words, her kindness, her tenderness,
her strong will, while on this earth, shall live on.
Mom is not gone.
Her memories will carry you on.

Don't cry, my son. Don't weep
I am not asleep.
I am not gone.
My love for you and those I touched lives on.
Think of all the good times, think of all the
conversations and all the quiet
times we spent together,
talking about this and that.

Cry if you wish, but not for very long.
You have things on this earth you must do.
Someday I will see you in heaven too.
Mom is not gone,
Never forget a mom's love.

Enjoy life, my son.
I am home now.
No more fear, no more tears,
I am in God's hands surrounded by angels,
family, and friends.
Mom is not gone.

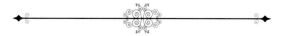

I AM A MAN

I'm a man when I realize that I've done something wrong and I can stand up and correct that wrong. I was raised as a boy to become a man, and I stand on those principles that were given to me and handed down by my dad.

I am a man when I break the codes between me and my dad, and in hindsight, I can see where I went wrong. I'm a man because I can correct that wrong because I know there is only one way to be a man.

I am a man when I take responsibility for all my actions. I am a man when I can raise my family, care for my family, provide for my family, and teach them, especially my kids, the principles that were taught to me by my dad. I am a man.

I am a man when I can stand up for what I believe in and fight for what's right. I am a man. I am a man when I can pick up the telephone and say, "I'm wrong, I'm sorry, please forgive me for what I have done." I am a man.

I am a man when I can look back on my teachings and I can look back on my education. I can look back on life experiences and pull from all those things the goodness that life has given me.

I am a man and I want the world to know. To all the men out there, stand up, accept your responsibilities, and do what's right and not what's wrong. You too, like me, will see and understand that here's nothing wrong with being a man. I am a man.

SYDNEY

Sydney is our granddaughter, clever as can be. She's got a smile that will knock you all the way from the east coast to the west coast and from north to south; that's Sydney. She can sense what's going on, and she'll come over and talk to you and say, "Grand-P, what's wrong?" I'll smile, keep going, and say, "Nothing, my dear," but that's Sydney. She is always trying to figure out what she can do. That's my granddaughter, Sydney. She has had a few losses in her young years on earth, but she is as tough as she can be. She has taken each one in stride. She talks about her mother being in heaven. She talks about her granny being in heaven too. At this writing she is only nine, but you would think she is twenty-two. That's my granddaughter, Sydney.

She is as clever as she can be. I like her sense of humor and her jokes too. She always finds something good to say even if it's at the end of the day. She has a smile out of this world and a sense of humor that I wish I had. She is a great kid and I hope that she grows up to be better than me because after all even at my age she has outwitted me. I guess I need to stop at this point because, if she reads this, I am sure she would come back with something off the wall to say to Grand-P, but all I'm going to say is "Sydney, Sydney, Sydney, it's you and me, Sydney."

A MAN OF HIS WORD

I've known this gentleman for thirty years, and whenever he says something, he means every word. He offers a suggestion or two not to criticize, like some would do, but he is a man of his word.

When he looks through a file or two, maybe three or four, he is looking to improve you. His soft voice is his way of life. Over the years he too has slowed down an inch or two, but when he speaks, he means well and always has. And never doubt this friend that I've known for thirty years, for what he says he means and what he says he'll do. We can all count on a friend like you—not one who criticizes and finds pleasure in doing so through and through but one who says to you, "Just think of this as a way to improve you." I'm glad to have a friend like you who can see my shortcomings in life, someone who can see that my heart is in my work and that I do my best to get the best results for those who depend upon me and you. I am grateful again to say, "I am glad to have a friend like you." Thank you, David.

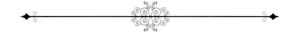

I'M GOING DOWN AND NEED A LIFT

I'm going down this highway and I need a lift. I'm traveling this world and I feel all alone. Don't know where to turn, but I do know I need a lift. I pick up the phone and call a friend and I say to them, "I'm going down and I need a lift because this world seems all against me." It is not you. When you feel your medical condition will never be right, you never look at the sun as a beautiful universe. You never look at the moon for the beauty of its light. You no longer see the trees for what they are worth. All you see is that you are going down, and I say to you, "I'm going down and I need a lift." Keep your head straight as can be. Smile at the world, and enjoy the sunshine, the rain, and the coldness of the wind; you're going down, but you got a lift. Lift your head, my friend, lift your head for he that gives will brighten your day. Look up in the clouds, my friend, you're not going down, you just thought you were . . . look up, look up because if you're going down I'm going to give you a lift, a lift, a lift, a lift.

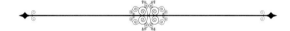

I AM YOUR FATHER . . . I AM YOUR DADDY

I am your father because of the nature from which you got here. I am your daddy because I show you things, teach you things, and give you love. I am your daddy because you look to me for guidance, love, and encouragement. I will never tell you something wrong. I will always try to explain things and why I say what I say and do what I do. I am your daddy.

Fathers sometimes are just what they are—fathers. They never take a role in their child's life with the exception of conception. A daddy will never forsake his child unless he is pushed to no end.

So we ask, what is a daddy? He is someone that you can talk to, someone who will listen, understand, and believe in your success. A daddy is someone who understands your pain, agony, and failures.

What is a daddy? A daddy is someone who spends time with his children, admits their failures in life, and shows you what not to do. A daddy's love and affection for his child should always be intact unless that child chooses to disrespect and be disobedient to his daddy. It is written in the Bible that a disobedient child shortens their days.

A daddy is a person who gives all his wisdom to you and continues to nurture and cultivate their relationship. A daddy smiles when his child smiles, cries when his child cries, hurts when his child hurts, and rejoices when his child rejoices.

There are many more things that a daddy does that compare him to a father, but I want you to know that it is okay even as the years go by and you think that you no longer need Daddy because you are now equipped with everything you need to face this world.

I want you to know that Daddy is not Daddy just to be Daddy. A real daddy will always give you his love, wisdom, trust, and all other things that he knows up until the day that he transcends from this world to the other. You can be sixty and he one hundred, but a true daddy loves his child. I want you to know that I was your father for only a short time and I became your daddy for a lifetime. I will love you and be there until the end. Never feel as though you cannot reach out to your daddy. He is your friend, guidance counselor, financial advisor, and spiritual advisor. He is many more things that I cannot even name. Just remember that he is Daddy, and he is Daddy for a reason.

MY FRIEND

We all have someone that we call friend. There are many definitions of a friend and some that I would never dream of. We look for different things in a person: how they treat us, how they have conversations with us, or how they act when we think they need something. A friend is someone that we can all on and in the end we say, "My friend."

My friend is someone that is special; someone who will be there through thick and thin, hell and high water; someone who will still be my friend; someone who, whether I do things all right or I do things all wrong, will still be my friend.

Over five decades, I have had many friends in my life; some I had to put to the test to find the truth, whether they were my friend, acquaintance, or enemy. I had to do those things to determine if they are my friends.

You are my friend when I need a hug, when I need someone to talk to. I don't like borrowing any funds, but if I did, you would give me half of your dime 'cause that shows me you are my friend. You are my friend when you make no judgments. You are my friend when you are listening and giving no answer. You are my friend when I ask you for your opinion. When I say, tell it like it is even if it hurts me. Just know that you are my friend. You are my friend no matter what, even when I take my last breath. I want to look up to you and say, "Thank you, my friend," thank you because you are my friend.

COUSIN BOB

Cousin Bob is really my second cousin, but if you met him you would see why everybody in town calls him Uncle Bob. He's a character. He's witty and he's funny.

Cousin Bob is from a little town in Middle Tennessee that is even harder to find on a map. He wrote a book or two, maybe three. Slowly he became known as Cousin Bob. He wears overalls no matter what the occasion is. I even think the day he leaves this world he will be packing his overalls. We call him Cousin Bob.

He knows his history. He can tell you who you are kin to and who you aren't. He can tell you where you have been and where you are going. All the while he's wearing a smile that could charm a snake. That's Cousin Bob.

Cousin Bob, what a man. If you see him on the street, he is going to strike up a conversation. If you go down to the Archives, he can tell you what you want to know and even what you didn't want to know. That's Cousin Bob.

Cousin Bob, what a guy. He says what he's going to do and does what he says. So when you are around town and see Cousin Bob with his overalls, just smile and say, "Come to see me." That's Cousin Bob.

OUR DAUGHTER

Our daughter is a unique female, always hidden behind that mirror and a reflection of her big brother. Our daughter got all the breaks. Many would say because she was the girl. Not sure if all of that is true, but a lot of it is. Our daughter has grown to be a lady, a lady that is quiet but well. Sometimes I don't like that about her, but what choice do I have.

Now as I reflect back, we gave her too many breaks. We didn't sit her down and talk to her the way parents should have. We didn't lay down the law. We didn't force many issues. We just let her evolve into the person that she is.

Our daughter has had her trials and tribulations. When tragedy struck, we all didn't know what to do. We had to put our trust and our faith in the good Lord and he came through. Our daughter discovered along the way all those so-called friends that she thought she had gone away. She had to come back full circle to be sure that the only people she could really count on were family.

Our daughter has made it up the hill. She may not ever sit on top as she once did, but she knows she has come a long way. She used to think hell was the only way out, but now she knows God is good all the time.

Our daughter, I don't like some of the decisions she makes and I keep my distance sometimes. I would rather be closer to her than I am, but she has that shorthand and it spells distance and I honor that; we honor that.

Our daughter, before I leave this world I'll have that last conversation and I know it's going to bring a tear or two, but it's something that I need to do. Our daughter, I would like to tell her as I write this poem, but the time is not right. I wish I could say more.

Our daughter, we will always love her until the end. She understands and she believes as we all do. She is not alone and she never has and never will be, and I hope she never forgets the true meaning of family, the true meaning of family. To our daughter, with love from your parents.

SIRAJ

Siraj is full of fun. He has that undaring attitude. Sometimes when he does not get his way, he says, "I'm not talking. I have nothing to say." He'll run to his room. He will wait a while, and when he comes flying through, he says, "Grand-P, you want to play with me?" Sometimes I say yes and sometimes I say no, and he'll look at me and say, "Why?" and I'll say, "Because of how you treat me." But I love that Siraj too.

When I get him outside on my four-wheeler, he is a different child. All he wants to do is speed, speed, speed. Slow down, Siraj, we are going to wreck, and he'll say "No, Grand-P, I'm driving through." That's Siraj. A daredevil not afraid of nothing. Siraj, I tried to teach him how to ride a bike and he got the general idea, but it was late at night. The next day I took off his training wheels and he said, "Grand-P, no training wheels, I won't ride my bike," and I said, "You won't be riding," and months later he's still not riding, but that's Siraj. He's cool, he's witty, he's charming at school, but when he's at home, huh, he's a devil or two. So beware of that little gentleman named Siraj. He's my grandson too.

SINGLE WITH KIDS DOES NOT MEAN THE END

I'm single with kids, no child support, no daddy support, and no outside support, except family. Single with kids does not mean the end.

I will make this journey along the way if and when I find that man who loves me and my kids and who can show me the way. I will always be able to say, "Single with kids doesn't mean the end." I'm single with kids and I'm trying to make it. I'm looking for ways to spread my wings. I'm looking for ways to tap into the resources that are within myself. I'm looking for ways in which I can improve the quality of life for me and my kids. Single with kids does not mean the end.

Yes, I am single with kids and I'm struggling just like many of you, but I won't give up. I keep trying and I'm grateful for that daddy of mine.

I know what it means to be on hard time. I know what it's like to not have a dime. I understand what life is all about, but I can say to you without a doubt, single with kids does not mean the end.

I'm going to make this journey alone if need be. I can't change what it is, but I can change what it can be. I'm going to make it one way or the other, but I want all of you to know, single with kids doesn't mean the end. I am who I am and I'm doing my best to make it. I know what it's like not to have a dime. But I also know what it's like to love my kids. They are my life and they are mine. I did what I did and don't regret it at all because I also know that God is going to take care of us. Single with kids doesn't mean the end and I will make it y'all.

MARRIAGE

Marriage in the ideal world is sacred between two people. They fall in love in most cases; they march down the aisle in other cases. For some, it's fine with a justice of the peace, a minister, or just a plain clerk of the courts to say "I do." So what is a marriage? Marriage's true intent is to be faithful to live a long life together, to do things, to grow, and to share all the disappointments, all the joys, and everything in between. So what's a marriage? Marriage is supposed to be a one-time thing, but people forget the reason they came together, the things they wanted to do, all their plans; some stay for the children, some stay for the status quo, some stay because of the money, and some stay because it's just a natural thing; but in the end, they are all unhappy. So I say, "What is a marriage?"

In marriage (ideally), you pool all your resources together, you remain independent, and you keep some of your good friends and let the bad ones go. You have kids, raise them, teach them, give them principles of life, prepare them for school and college, and prepare them for everyday life. You look forward in some cases, but not all, for grandkids that are coming along, and then you say, "I'm saving all our money for the grandkids." Then we ask ourselves when it's all over, "What is a marriage?"

A marriage is between two people. They dream of being on the same page and knowing where they are going. There are things that cause a marriage to derail itself. Some folks make a decision to put the marriage back on track, whether it be going through counseling or saying "I'm sorry, I'm only human" or "It's my fault," "his/her fault," or "our fault." But either way we still ask the question "What is a marriage?"

A marriage, when it comes to an end in many cases, hearts are broken. There are things that you must divide between the two. I want this and I want that, she wants this and she wants that, he wants this and he wants that, or "I gave this to you when . . ." So when it's all over, there is no need to go through the fighting; there is no need to be ugly about anything. There were more good days than there were bad days, and now, we have just reached a point where we have decided the intersections no longer intersect. The circle is no longer, no longer closed; the square has an opening, and the rectangle is pointed down instead of up; so in the end, a marriage should be "Let's remain friends."

If we have young kids, do what's in the best interest of them. That is the ideal way to think to end a marriage. Do the right thing, and if not, you deal with it. So when it's all said and done, there is no need to hate. Hate only brings on more hate. I have always said and I will continue to say until the day I die, "There is good in everything that's not good, you just have to look for it."

So if a marriage must come to an end, try to remain positive, keep your head up, unwrap your heart, live again, be cautious, do what you didn't do the first time around, and live. That is what a marriage should be about: to live if it should come to an end.

MEME

Meme was this very young attractive lady that I met when I was a senior in high school. Weighed every bit of one hundred pounds wet but has some beautiful, gorgeous long legs. As time went by, I left the city for a while and I came back and got myself a date with Meme.

We dated for about three weeks and overseas I went. We wrote each other love letters and talked about having a life together and all those good things that was necessary to keep me and Meme together.

We fell in love and I returned home and as I recall that was leap year, and that year Meme wanted to get married. Of course, after conferring with my dear mother, a decision was made to do just that. We got married and we both went overseas to a beautiful land by the sea. We began to grow together and enjoy a wonderful life, and as life would have it, we had a son and we enjoyed all those fun years in a foreign land, a beautiful place by the sea, just me and Meme.

Some thirty-seven years later, we have had our ups and downs, but that's the way marriages work. More good days than bad, but I am still in love with my Meme.

She is as sweet as she can be, but in her old age, she has decided she does not want to travel with me. She stays behind, which is fine, and she is content and I am on the road looking for this and that to bring back.

I can say without a doubt, it was love at first sight, and even those who may choose not to believe this, I want you to know, don't have any doubt that that's my Meme. As warm as she can be, gentle and kindhearted too. The things that she does for me is because she is Meme.

We do not fuss about the small stuff and we plan ahead, but every now and then, she may agree to travel with me, but in the end, it's just me and Meme.

I love you no matter what I do or how I act, and anything that goes down in between, you know for sure without a doubt that deep down inside, I still truly love, my Meme.

DAVID

David, you are my friend and you are my brother. I met you some twenty-plus years ago, and even today, I wonder where you are. I call your cell phone and you don't answer, I call the home phone and you don't answer, I leave you a message and you don't reply, so I wonder why.

I've carried you through thick and thin and I stood by you every time. I never asked anything of you, but on this day I ask, "David, where are you and where have you been?"

I don't know if I should pick up the phone and try again or if I should come knocking on your door and ask you, "Where in the hell have you been?" David, you are my brother and you are my friend. I didn't have to extend my hand, but for the love of God and the love of man, I knew when I saw you. You really needed a true friend, but, David, where are you?

I don't know where you are, but I do know where you've been. Now I'm wondering should I try again. You are my brother and you are my friend, but I have to ask just one more time, "David, where have you been?"

If I don't call or come around, then you will wonder, where is my friend? I can only try again, then after that, David, I am going to have to ask, "Are you really my friend?" and I say, "David, David, where have you been?"

SISTER

You are the only sister God gave us. I don't know why people cause so much confusion between us, especially when I said nothing at all about you. I'm not angry, I'm not mad, and I'm not upset at you at all! I gave you space as this brother often does.

When Mom left, it left this family divided. The day is going to come when all our burdens will be lifted from us. Let's hope that we all have made peace. I don't like feeling I'm living all alone. I have fought my illness for over twenty-one years in all, but the last few months, I've had thoughts of ending it all, but I'm stronger than that even though my mind and body is under attack, but then that fight comes back because there are people like you who love me. So, sis, don't let others, no matter who they are, divide us at all. There is no need to pick up the telephone and call. I respect your space and I can say you are not all alone. I will never forsake Christmas, your birthday, Valentine's, or Mother's Day. God only gave us one sister, and no matter what, I will not forsake that along my way. The thought of all this has caused me some pain because my body and my mind are vulnerable these days. I've cried my tears and I'm sorry our upbringing didn't bring us closer. We're getting older and some of us will never give in or change our ways. So for those siblings who do not desire change, mind your own business.

Sis, you are the only sister God gave us. Don't be so distant. We are all getting older. I know I cannot bear the burdens for us all. I love you, and like me, let's not feel like we are all alone. I know I'll make it through it all.

I will continue to give you your space that's just the way we are. No matter what the situation may be along the way, I will never forsake Christmas, your birthday, Valentine's, or Mother's day. God only gave us one sister, and no matter what I will not forsake that along the way. I love you, sis, and that's all.

I AM PROUD TO HAVE A FATHER LIKE I DO

I am proud to have a father like I do because he has always been there for me through and through. When I have given him grief or did something wrong, he may have gotten angry or not said anything at all, but I am glad that I have a father like you.

I am glad that I have a father like you because you taught me to have character, respect, honesty, love for God, and many more attributes that I cannot name. But I am glad to have a father like you.

I am glad to have a father like you who is understanding, has a great sense of humor, never gets rattled, and is not afraid to say what's on his mind or make it clear to you that you are not welcome.

Sometimes, I say, "I don't understand why my father does what he does, or says what he says, or takes a stand when it just doesn't seem right, but I am glad to have a father like you." I am glad to have a father like you and to know that you love me and care for me, and you will always be there for me. You will always tell me what's right and what's wrong and not judge me too harshly because I know deep down inside that it was the military that carved you out and made you a man for that too; I am glad to have a father like you.

I am glad to have a father like you that extends your heart and your love through and through to others that don't even know you or sometimes that you just met.

I am glad to have a father like you because I have seen the things that you do, and now that I am older and wiser, I can always say, "Until the day that I die, I am glad to have a father like you."

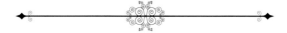

MY FRIEND CB

CB has always been my friend. From the time we began to associate as the years went by, she was still my friend. My friend CB, like me, has gone through lots of trials and tribulations. Sometimes it felt like it was the end of the road, but we remained friends through it all.

My friend CB has never left me. She has never been critical of what I did or what I didn't do and has tried to remain neutral through the years gone by through and through.

My friend CB and I have shared many stories about what happened in my life and her life as well as in the lives of all the folks that have touched me and her too.

My friend CB, to this day, a quarter century later, still remains my friend. We will be friends to the end. That's my friend CB, never judging me!

Inspirational

LIFE CHANGES IN AN INSTANT

Life changes in an instant when you think
everything is going great.
Something happens.
Life changes in an instant.

When you rise in the morning, planning your day,
thinking nothing can go wrong,
something happens.
Life changes in an instant.

When you think your relationship
is on track with love, happiness, respect, and trust,
then something happens.
Life changes in an instant.

When you have a moment to reflect,
the mind wanders from good to not so good
and back, your heart flutters and your
soul rejoices knowing that
your life changes in an instant.

No matter what happens, good or bad,
happy or sad, love or no love,
something or nothing, dreams or no dreams,
money or no money, either way,
something happens and
life changes in an instant.

TODAY

Today, I begin my journey, not sure where I am going or what I am going to do, but I do know today I shall smile. I shall warm a heart or two. I shall have conversations because today is today. Today I look at life differently because it has so much to offer. I take all the good out of the badness and turn it into sweetness. I turn tears into drops of gold. I turn blood into a red steady flow of love. Today will always be a day to be remembered.

A day to laugh about, a day to smile about, a day to think about, a day to remember, but it is a day. It is a day that God Almighty has made for us. So on this day, just like every day, I wake up thankful that he has allowed me to rise. I go to bed at night and I am thankful that he allowed me to go through the day. Today, I am glad that you crossed my path and that you helped make today what it is.

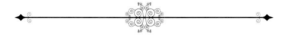

JUST BELIEVE

Just believe that you can do anything that you want to. Never give up when everything seems all against you. Just believe because there is hope and there is love. Just believe that today is new, and never forget God's love. Just believe that when you are down that you are going to get up or that pain that you might be having today will go away.

Just believe that you were put in this world for a purpose and that God made no mistake. Given the opportunity of today, you can make a difference in the lives of those that you see and those that have you touched. Just believe and things will come your way. Just believe that, as you end this day, there will be joy in the morning, and believe that whatever you dreamed can come true. Never forgetting that God made you, and with him, you must believe. I say to you, just believe, just believe in God, and he will carry you through.

I'M TIRED

My body is tired, my mind is tired, my muscles are tired, and I'm just plain tired. Medication relieves the pain, but only momentarily, and then my body resumes the position of being tired.

I'm tired. I'm tired of all the pain, agony, tears, and feeling that there is no reason to carry on. Some would call that a sense of despair, but to me, twenty-one years of this, I'm tired. I'm tired. I'm tired.

I have a cocktail of medications that I believe is playing with the mind. Playing with the mind to the point that it tells me it will never go away. That little voice says, "End it, end it, end it, the pain is not going away." So I'm tired, tired, tired.

I struggle this time around. It came out of hibernation on or near July 10, 2010. It has been kicking my butt, I will not hide it, but it has caused me to be tired, tired, tired.

Sometimes I ask myself, "What can I do?" and then I answer myself, "There is nothing I can do." I listen to the doctors and I do what they say, but still at the end of the day, I'm tired. I'm tired. I'm tired. I may call up a friend to hear their voice or ask for some reinforcements of sorts but never tell them what's really on my mind because they wouldn't believe that I was that kind. They wouldn't believe that the hard shell that I have displayed for years has a bitter softness that makes me almost unreal. But I'm tired, I'm tired, I'm tired. They send me to see a psychiatrist and he's friendly, but sometimes I really don't want to share what's really inside of me because I know that anything that I say, anything that I do, or even anything that I write might someday show up because there are some things a psychiatrist refuses to keep out of sight. I will deal with this more openly than before, but that still does not relieve me of the pain that's galore. All I can say is what I'm saying now: "I'm tired. I'm tired. I'm tired." Maybe as the years go by and I slow down, I can only think that the pain will follow me and hopefully it will slow down too. I'm not giving up just yet, but there have been periods lately when I have really said, "Why fight it?" and then that inner part of me says, "You're not that kind. You fight, my friend, you fight." But even today, I'm as tired as I can be. The body is tired, the mind is tired, the soul is getting tired, and my desire to fight is getting tired too. But I'm going to hang on a little while longer because, while I'm getting tired, and tired, and tired, I'm not ready to go. So good-bye for now; I'm not gone so stay tuned to my family and friends.

IT IS HUMAN TO CRY

We come into this world crying like a baby because we know no other. We grow up to be young men and young women, and when something happens, sometimes we fail to cry. We fail to cry because we don't want others to see that we are human, so it is human to cry. There will be times that we cannot control the tears that flow. There will be situations that will go untold, but we cannot control the tears that flow; but it's human to cry.

We are taught, especially being a man, that you don't cry; you just suck it in. But it's human to cry. There are times when illness comes, kids have disappointed us, and work is not what we want it to be, and there are times when bad things happen to good people, and it's still human to cry.

I know we like to control the flow of the tears, but that is something we cannot control even if it goes on for years. We may stop, we may heal, and we may carry on, but there is going to be something along the way that will tell us again that you cannot control the flow of your tears. It is human to cry. So as you read this and you reflect back on your life, even if you cried many tears in the past, don't be embarrassed. That is the way of life because after all we cannot control the flow of tears. It is okay to cry; it is okay to cry a tear. It is okay to be human and cry.

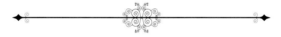

I AM MOVED BY YOU

I am moved by you because of the way you carry yourself. You show dominance and independence. I am moved by you.

I am moved by you because of your desire to want to live and to accomplish many things in life. I am moved by you because you want a college education, a nice home, nice clothing, a warm compassionate and intimate love, and maybe a husband or wife and children. I am moved by you.

I am moved by you because of the way that you think, the way that you handle conflicts, and the way that you are able to bring people and situations together. I am moved by you.

I am moved by you because of how you carry yourself. How you carry yourself in this big old world.

Always understanding, you must take care of yourself first. The way you reach out to others and the way you show those around you including family that you care. I am moved by you.

I am moved by you because of who you are, where you want to go, what you want to be in life, and how you plan to get there. You're determined to beat all odds and to show the world that you are who you are, and with the help of God, you will reach the top and achieve all things that you have conceived with the help of God Almighty. I am moved by you.

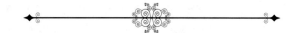

YOU DON'T UNDERSTAND ME

You don't understand me because of the things that I do or the things that I want. You don't understand me because I refuse to stand or sit there and not be moved. You don't understand me because I want the best out of life. I will make whatever sacrifices necessary to make things happen. You don't understand me.

You don't understand me because you don't want to understand me, but you look for fault in order to cause a conflict. You don't understand me because you want to keep me down and not allow me to spread my wings. You don't understand me. You're jealous because I believe and because I refuse to let anything stop me. You included. Therefore, you do not understand me.

You do not understand me because I have a spiritual connection, and spiritual connection protects me. I pray to my God every day that I'm here on earth that he will always protect me, give me the understanding, direct me, and show me where I am weak so that I may become strong. You don't understand me. You don't understand me not because you can't. It is because you won't. You don't understand me because I'm headed north and you're headed south, and life will tell me again, "You don't understand me."

You don't understand me not because you can't. It's because you won't. I must move on and achieve the things that I want. I must stand tall in this universe and I must follow the word of God. If you want to understand me you too must come aboard, and if not, it is clear that you unfortunately and sadly do not understand me!

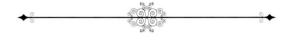

BRIDGE OVER TROUBLED WATERS

Sometimes we are faced with the most difficult situations in the world. We don't know whether to turn left or right or stop at the stop sign or at an intersection. It is called bridge over troubled waters. When we are faced with something that we have done and we're not sure how to handle it, when we're faced with a situation of something we've done, and we find ourselves balled up in a knot with emotions of all sorts and we still don't know whom to talk to, then it is called a bridge over troubled waters.

We're not perfect in this world, and what we do sometimes is not always right and not always wrong. We are taught right from wrong, but sometimes our emotions get involved and we can't see, can't hear, and can't feel; we just act. When this happens, it is called bridge over troubled waters.

We cry our eyes out and we are sad to for what we did. We regret all the pain, agony, and anything else in between that we did. We know that we cannot change or turn back the hands of time, but we know going forward that we don't have to ride that bridge over troubled waters again. So to those of you who feel that you have driven over and or created a bridge over troubled waters, face whatever it may be, search your soul, and ask God to forgive you for whatever wrong you did, and I can assure you that there will never be another bridge over troubled waters.

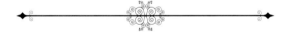

I DON'T KNOW WHAT TO DO, LORD

I don't know what to do, Lord. I'm confused, and I have no sense of direction of what else to do. I tried to call a friend or two and got no answer. I tried to rely on myself, but, Lord, I don't know what to do.

Lord, the rent is due, my government subsidies have been cut, the cable is about to be whacked, and I have no telephone, but I do know, Lord, I have you. But I still don't know what to do.

Lord, I'm running low of money in the bank, so I feel as if the love that I once had has gone too. I reach back into my heart and into my mind, for I know there is something or someone out there for me, but,

Lord, I don't know what to do.

Lord, I've given my all and I've tried everything that I know how to do. I say to you, "I've called all my friends some relatives too." I've called strangers that I did not know and now, Lord, I come back to you and I ask a question: "Lord, what am I supposed to do?"

Lord, what am I supposed to do now that I've cried all my tears and I have no more tears to shed? Now that I have no one else to turn to and I'm about to lose everything that I've worked so hard for? Lord, the only thing that I know to do is pray, pray, pray, and pray. Lord, bless me so that I will know what to do.

SMILE

I smile in the morning, I smile at noon, I smile in the evenings, and I smile at night. All I do is smile.

I smile because I'm happy. I smile because I see the sun, I see the moon, I see the clouds, and I see everything around me. I smile.

I smile because it is the right thing to do whether I know you or you might be a stranger. I smile. I smile because it gives me joy. I nod and I smile to acknowledge you. I smile.

I smile when I'm down and out. I smile when I'm in pain, but I still smile. I've learned that it takes fewer muscles to smile than it does to frown. I smile. I smile because the world is a wonderful place to be, and I smile because the good Lord allowed me to rise today and see. I smile.

I want you to know today there's nothing wrong with the word that says, "I smile, I smile, and I smile."

I WANT TO BE LIKE YOU

I want to be like you because you're somebody. You've shown the world that you would stand up and that you would voice your opinion for folks who cannot. I want to be like you.

I want to be like you because you give the strength and the sign that you're not weak. I want to be like you because you are an example of what the world should be about. I want to be like you because you stand for righteousness and you stand for belief in mankind. I want to be like you. I want to be like you because you have compassion in your heart, you have love in your voice, and you have a mind that can draw people together at the worst times. I want to be like you. I want to be like you because I know, being like you, I can help others and I can say that you set the example and you set the bar. I want to be able to say, "I know how you are." I want to be like you. I want to be like you because there's no other. There are not two of you, just one, and I like the examples of being like you, so I want to say again, "I want to be like you."

DON'T GIVE UP ON YOUR DREAMS

Don't give up on your dreams, for sometimes dreams are all we have. God gave us the ability to dream and to wonder, and He gave us the ability to understand. Don't give up on your dreams.

It's like playing baseball: you might get a fastball, curveball, or knuckleball, or it may be a slow curve, but don't give up on your dreams simply because life has thrown you a curve. Don't give up on your dreams.

God gave us the ability to do the things that we want to do. It is often said, if you can conceive it, you can achieve it, so don't give up on your dreams.

No matter what the situation may be in life, no matter where you are, you may have been on the top and fallen afar, you may be on the bottom and trying to crawl up, but I still say, "Don't give up on your dreams."

Dreams, dreams, dreams—they can be the beginning of something beautiful in life, so don't give up on your dreams. Don't give up on wanting what you thought about all your life and say, "I can't." There is no such word as *can't*. There is a word that says "I can." So I say to you, "If you believe you can, it will happen." God loves you, and I love you too. So no matter who you are, no matter where you are in life, don't give up on your dreams.

WE ARE HUMAN TOO

If I am sitting on the other side of the desk or sitting behind the desk, it doesn't matter. I'm human too. We don't know how that person feels. Sometimes those who sit behind the desk and those who sit on the other side don't know whether to talk, walk, crawl, or hide, but we are human too.

Sometimes we take our profession as seriously as can be. We make the best decisions that we can foresee, and sometimes we are right on target and other times we are off base, but it only goes to show that we are human too.

No matter what we do, whether we laugh, smile, or we cry and shed a tear or two, we are human too.

Sometimes we make decisions, sometimes right and sometimes wrong. Sometimes we come to a conclusion that's not right at all. Sometimes we give advice, but we are really not sure at all, but we give it our best and we can say we are human too. We must always be aware of those out there who are not sure if we are human at all. Sometimes we walk tall with our chests stuck out, and other times we walk small, knowing that we might just fall. We're not sure at the end of the day, if everything we did or everything we might have said was right or wrong, but one thing is for sure, I am human too. As you read this, I hope that you can reflect back on your life whether it be just now, last night, last month, or last year. Whether all the decisions we made were right or wrong, we must walk away with one thing if nothing at all. We are human too.

THE SUN

The sun has come up as bright as it can be. Riding down the highway, it's peeking, I can see. It is really bright; maybe I need to change my sunglasses—I'm not sure yet! I go around the hill, I go around the curve, and I think I'm coming up on a mountain. The sun disappears for a second or two, but I can still say, "The sun, the sun is bright and it's hot." It's peeking through the clouds and what a beautiful glow it has. It's called the sun. The sun lets you know when it rises, and it lets you know when it sets, but it's called the sun. The sun—without it we would be lost. We need the warmth of the sun, we need the glow of the sun, and we need its beauty as it sneaks in between the clouds like no other. Maybe tonight we'll get a chance to see the moon because it must be the cousin to the sun. The sun is a beautiful thing to see. The sun—without it where would we be? The sun . . . the sun . . . the sun.

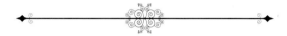

I'M LEAVING WORK

I'm leaving work as I always do. It's dark outside and I must make a stop or two. I've had a conversation with a coworker of mine and I enjoyed that time. I know life is what it is and we can't change it all, but it's fun leaving work knowing that you haven't lost it all. I'm leaving work now and I see a car here and a car there; it's pretty dark outside. Sometimes it blows your mind!

The glow of headlights and the glow of taillights let me know that it's dark outside. I just left work and I am going home to relax now. As I reflect back on today, it has been a good one. I am going to say that there is always a tomorrow, and we must make the best of today because tomorrow is just tomorrow.

I am going home now and I hope that I have made a difference in someone's life today; I hope that my words of wisdom found a place somewhere in my coworker's heart. And as they travel the highways and byways and become older, they will reflect back and say, "I remember when an old fellow said to me, "Always be encouraged and never satisfied even when it's at the end of the day. If you don't know where you are going, any road will take you there." As I leave and it's dark outside, I am going home to finish my day. No matter what we do and no matter what we don't do, as long as we can live with an understanding upfront, it's better than a misunderstanding down the road. I am going home now to relax, and I just want those who read this to just sit back and say, "What a wise guy!" He shared his wisdom and he shared it well, but he has gone home to relax, relax, and relax forever.

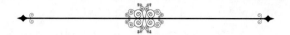

A CHANGE IS GOING TO COME

On a warm December day in the year of 2000, a change is going to come. I see the beauty of sunny skies and the joy of clouds. The nakedness of the trees or the trees with no leaves, a change is going to come. I see a woman so far in the distance as she reaches for the sun, dreams of reaching the moon, and craves to find that loved one who will love her just as she is. A change is going to come.

In the morning when it's cold, we wait for the sunshine. When the sun does not come out, we see a cloudy day. But I see a lady, and no matter whether it's raining, cold, cloudy, or sunny, there is a smile at the end like the beauty of rainbow; a change is going to come.

We dream sometimes; we look into outer space and just wonder. We think about what tomorrow will bring. We try to wash away all the badness and all the sadness, all the bad things, but we know a change is going to come and a change is on its way.

As you lie in the bed at night and the memories begin to flow from the left to right lobe before you know it's all over the heart and the body, a big smile with a glow. We know a change is going to come. A change is on its way. When the day is over and when the day is done, you shall retreat back to a place of comfort she knows; she knows that there is love, she knows that there is happiness, and she knows that there is a future; she knows that a change is going to come, and a change is on its way.

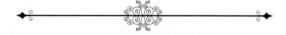

I'M NOT ALONE

I am not alone. I am not alone in this big old world. Sometimes it seems so small, but I'm not alone. Sometimes I look around and feel like I have been swallowed up, but I'm not alone. Sometimes when I am sitting at my desk, trying to get all the things done that I know that I can't, I'm not alone. Sometimes I ride down the highway for long hours . . . long hours . . . but I'm not alone. Sometimes I lie in bed at night and my mind begins to wonder, it goes from over there to over here and back again, but I'm not alone.

When I cry at night, when I hurt at night and the pain won't go away, I feel like I want to give up, but I'm not alone. I tell others that life is good and we can fight this battle, one day at a time. I'm not alone.

When I go see my doctor, he tells me what I don't want to hear; I'm not alone. When I think about all the other folks in the world that are in worse situations than I am—those who can't get up, those who can't talk, those whose family has abandoned them, and those whose folks don't care about them—I'm not alone and neither are they.

No matter the place, no matter the time, no matter the city, no matter where on this big round earth, I'm not alone. I want you to know today, as you read this, you are not alone. You are not alone. God Almighty is always with us. No matter where we are, he created us and he said he will not forsake us, so I'm not alone.

OPRAH

As beautiful as she can be, she got her start just north of me. While it didn't last long and she moved on, she proved to the world that she was good as thee. She is now known as the queen of TV.

Millions listen every day to see, to listen, and to learn what's new from her. She has announced that she'll quit showbiz because she has made millions since she moved from north of me. Her energy is like no other, and she gives those that are trying to make it a chance because she remembers what happened to the queen of TV in Nashville, Tennessee.

She never forgot her roots. Her generosity has been felt by millions. When her time comes and she's off the air, I think all of you need to remember from where she came from and all the kind things that she has done, especially for the kids in South Africa. Oprah, the queen of TV, wherever you go and whatever you do, there are millions and millions of folks who love you too. You've done well and I've been a follower just like all the others. Good-bye to that African queen of TV—Oprah! Good-bye.

WHY ME, LORD?

Why me, Lord? I don't know. After all these years, you have now tapped my soul. You're having me express a talent that you have given, a talent that I have had on the shelf, gathering dust for so long. So I say, "Why me, Lord?" I don't know but I will follow You.

Why me, Lord? To express in words that might help someone along the way. It may be someone who had a bad day. It may be someone who had bad news. It may be someone who needs to just relax and reflect. I don't know, Lord, but I say, "Why me?"

I will accept Your challenge. I will continue to do these things that you want me to do, and if this writing is a way to reach others because You chose me, I will do so, Lord, but I say, "Why me?"

Sometimes this brings a tear to my face and sometimes I don't understand it. Sometimes it just comes and goes in the wee hours of the night and during the day. You send me a title, Lord, and You say "Write" and I comply. Lord, I will do Your work, I will do Your teachings through my writings, but I will say, "Why me, Lord, why me?"

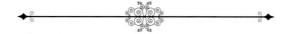

I HAVE THE HEART OF A LION

I have the heart of a lion because I do things that others would not dream of. I open my hands, my heart, home, wallet, and all the other things that are necessary to please mankind. I have the heart of a lion.

I have the heart of a lion because I think about what life is today and how I have been blessed. I think about those who are less fortunate, and I donate my time and my money to help them along the way. I cry and I care about the human race. I have the heart of a lion.

I have the heart of a lion because I have been taught to give and not receive. I have been taught the golden rule. I have been taught right from wrong. I have been taught to forgive and to forget. I have been taught the Ten Commandments. I have been taught to live and let live and to love my brothers and my sisters.

I have the heart of a lion.

I have the heart of a lion because I see the injustice in the world today and I make every effort to correct the injustices and to right all wrongs. I will go that extra mile for someone that I don't know and give them a helping hand when everyone else says no. I have the heart of a lion!

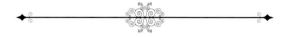

JUST A WOMAN

I am just a woman with a warm heart, a heart that many say shouldn't be because, each time I open my heart, it becomes shattered in pieces. I am just a woman trying to do the right thing and do the things that I was taught to do, and the things that I know are right.

I am just a woman hoping I can make a difference in someone's life. Whether it is a young boy, young girl, friend, relative, or stranger, I am just a woman trying to do the right thing.

I am just a woman that has been touched from the spiritual side of my God, and with that, I know I shall and I will never ever be alone. I am just a woman trying to make it in this world and I pray every day for guidance, love, and strength along the way. I am just a woman.

I am just a woman doing the right thing and trying to make the right decisions and living the golden rule. I know, despite all obstacles in the world today and those that may pass my way, I am going to remain a strong firm, determined and independent woman. For I am just a woman!

WHAT IF?

What if I had no one in this world to turn to? I would be a sad and lost soul. But if there was no one on this earth with me I would still be happy because I have the Lord.

What if I had no friends? We all want friends—good friends, bad friends, and friends who are yet to be friends. Sometimes our friends move, die, or change their ways and you feel all alone, but you are not alone in this world. The Lord will always be your friend. What if I lost everything of material value in this world and I had nowhere to go, no place to stay. What would I do? I would turn to the Lord because he is my friend through hell and high water. He is your friend.

What if I felt the burden of life from all the things that have happened to me: I am sick, I lost my job, I have little money, and these burdens are just too much to bear? Turn to the Lord because he is the friend of all friends, lawyer of all lawyers, and doctor of all doctors. He is the comforter to all those who need comfort. What if?

I can say without a doubt that there is no need to what if—except life, all its ups and downs, its burdens and joys, and all the things in between. If you trust and believe in the Lord and follow His teachings, the Lord shall make a way. In the end, what-ifs are wiped out and they are replaced by hallelujah, hallelujah, hallelujah, amen.

WHAT IS A LIE

A lie is not telling the truth. No matter how you turn it, fold it, bundle it, and roll it, a lie is a lie.

A lie even if you try to put a new truth on it or stretch the truth, it's still a lie. What is a lie? When you begin to stretch the imagination to where it is not supposed to be stretched. When to make excuses of this, that, or the other. When you know right from wrong and wrong is wrong. That's a lie.

A lie to some people is a way of life. They have always lied about everything. Lie to be accepted, to look good, to hear themselves talk, to try to gain an edge in a game or a relationship or two—but it is still a lie.

A lie is when you hide from the real truth for it may hurt you and you do not want to face reality head on like a collision with a car—*bam!* And a lie is really what it is. Plainly spoken, a lie is not the truth.

I say to all of you, a lie is not the truth and some folks lie just to lie. I hope that you are able to see as you become wiser and older with maturity, the difference between the truth and a lie and right from wrong. So I ask the question "What is a lie?"

WHEN I LAY MY HEAD DOWN AT NIGHT

When I lay my head down at night, I see You, Lord. I see You in the nighttime and I see You in the daytime. I think about You, Lord, all the time.

When I lay my head down at night to sleep, I think about You, Lord, I think about You. In times of trouble, I think about You. In times of joy, I think about You. In times of sadness and despair, I think about You, Lord.

I think about You, Lord, and all the things that You do. I think about You, Lord, because I know You will carry me through. I know times seem hard and we don't know what to do, but, Lord, I think about You.

I think about You as I look out and see all the beautiful creations in this world—the things that I have always wanted to see and the things that I know I will never ever see—but, Lord, I think of about You.

I think about You, Lord, when I lay down at night, I think of You. I pray to You, Lord, because I know You. Despite all things You will carry me through.

I pray, Lord, that You will always be with me and that You will show me, teach me, guide me and be there in the midnight hour when I am filled with despair. I know, Lord, You will be there because You will carry me through.

When I lay my head down at night, I think about You, Lord. I think about You and I am blessed. I am blessed because of all the things that You do. I think about You, Lord, I think about You.

TEACH ME TO UNDERSTAND YOU

Teach me to understand you because I don't know how.
I could try on my own, but I would screw it up.

Teach me to love you the way you like.
Teach me to hold you without boundaries.
Teach me to understand you.

Teach me to read your eyes, your expressions,
your emotions and your thoughts.

Teach me to be passionate in ways
never experienced before.
Teach me to understand you.

Teach me to smile, to relax and enjoy life.
Teach me in ways that I never thought of before.
Teach me new things. I want to learn.
Teach me to understand you
so that I can love and care
for you for the rest of my life.

Just teach me with your love.

LIFE IS GOOD

Life is good. You rise each morning and see the sun. You inhale the Lord's fresh air and you exhale with the spirit. Life is good.

Life is good when you feel the spirit of self, looking for today, living for tomorrow, and planning for the future. Life is good.

Life is good when you think you have problems, and in a blink of an eye, your problems are gone. Life is good when you know that dark cloud has been lifted.

Life is good just knowing you have made a difference in someone's life. Just to see and share into a person's happiness, to laugh together, to share together, and to reflect upon life together. Never forget, life is good no matter what.

Life is good when you can feel the love of another person, the love of God, the love of nature, and the love of two hearts, two minds, and two souls. Life is good.

Life is good when you can feel calmness around you and when life comes together like no other. Life is good.

Life is good today, tomorrow, and the future. Thank God for all our blessings and life shall forever be good.

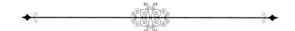

WORKING IN A MAN'S WORLD

She is working in a man's world with expectations higher than her male coworkers, and surprised to them she exceeded all expectations while working in a man's world.

She is well prepared to take on her fight, her beliefs, and her duty to God. Months went by and she added years to her career and the good old boys couldn't understand how she succeeded while working in a man's world.

Working in a man's world, she proved to the world that trusting in herself, believing in her oath, committed to helping the less fortunate, prepared to give her all, never questioning why she chose her profession. She succeeded while working in a man's world.

Years later she's on top of her profession. Wow! How times have changed. Honored, respected, persevered, and on top of the world. She succeeded while working in a man's world!

I CAN CHANGE

I can change because change is good.
I can change not for you but for myself.
I can change 'cause change means a better
life for myself and my family.

I can change 'cause doing nothing means
the same old thing, same old face,
same old scenery. . . . To not change,
I lose everything!

I can change 'cause the world is waiting for a change.
I can change because change is good—good
for the body, good for the mind, good
for the soul, and good for love.

I can change because I can see things differently.
I can change because I have many good reasons
to change. Reason to care, reason to share,

reason to love, reason to see what darkness left
me, reason to rise above, and reason to show
myself and world, I can change.

I can change, if that means leaving my old
friends behind, if they cannot accept my change.
I can change because God is good, and without my
belief in Him, I am lost today, tomorrow, and forever.
I will change; I will never look back.

I can change because there are others who believe in
me like never before, a belief so strong that life
today is new.

I can change. I can stop all my bad habits. I can modify
my life. I can see the future. I can smile with joy. I
can cry for happiness. I can love like never before.
I can see my children grow from my change and
my love. I can change.

I can change, I can accept change, and I can do anything
I want to do or be in life. I can and I will change.

Believe in me and I will show you, I believe in change. I can and I will change from this
moment forward. Thank you for believing in me. Today is the first day of my new life!

I believe in change.
Change is good for the body, mind, and soul!

I BELIEVE IN CHANGE . . .

Printed in the United States
By Bookmasters